Animal Look-Alikes

Hares
and Rabbits

Joanne Mattern

RED
CHAIR
· PRESS ·

Animal Look-Alikes is produced and published by Red Chair Press:

Red Chair Press LLC   PO Box 333   South Egremont, MA 01258-0333

www.redchairpress.com

About the Author

Joanne Mattern is the author of nearly 350 books for children and teens. She began writing when she was a little girl and just never stopped! Joanne loves nonfiction because she enjoys bringing science topics to life and showing young readers that nonfiction is full of compelling stories! Joanne lives in the Hudson Valley of New York State with her husband, four children, and several pets, which look nothing alike!

Publisher's Cataloging-In-Publication Data

Names: Mattern, Joanne, 1963-

Title: Hares and rabbits / Joanne Mattern.

Description: [South Egremont, Massachusetts] : Red Chair Press, [2018] | Series: Animal look-alikes | Interest age level: 006-010. | Includes science vocabulary, fun facts, and trivia about each type of animal. | "Core content library." | Includes bibliographical references. | Summary: "Long floppy ears. Big teeth. Running or hopping. Is it a rabbit or a hare? Learn how these popular and cuddly animals are alike and how they differ!"--Provided by publisher.

Identifiers: LCCN 2016947286 | ISBN 978-1-63440-212-5 (library hardcover) | ISBN 978-1-63440-217-0 (ebook)

Subjects: LCSH: Hares--Juvenile literature. | Rabbits--Juvenile literature. | CYAC: Hares. | Rabbits.

Classification: LCC QL737.L32 M38 2018 (print) | LCC QL737.L32 (ebook) | DDC 599.32--dc23

Illustrations by Tim Haggerty.

Photo credits: Shutterstock except for the following: p. 7: © Andy Rouse/Minden Pictures; p. 12: © Michael and Patricia Fogden/Minden Pictures; p. 26: © John Cancalosi/NPL/Minden Pictures

Printed in Canada

102017 1P FRNS18

Table of Contents

Hare or Rabbit?

Look, it's a rabbit! Or is it a hare? Sometimes it is hard to tell these two animals apart. Many people think rabbits and hares are the same. Although there are some things about these two animals that are the same, there are also many things that are different. Let's find out more about hares and rabbits!

Warm, Furry Mammals

Hares and rabbits are both **mammals**. Mammals have a backbone. Most mammals give birth to live babies. Baby mammals need their mothers to take care of them. Mother mammals feed their babies with milk from their bodies.

One of the most important facts about mammals is that they are warm-blooded. Mammals can control their body temperature. Their bodies stay the same temperature no matter what the temperature is around them. Remember, you are a mammal too. Your body temperature stays about 98.6 degrees F (37 C) no matter the air temperature.

Power Word: Lagomorphs are plant-eating animals with two rows of front teeth. Pikas are the only other lagomorph family. Have you seen a pika?

This European hare mother is nursing her young.

Scientists used to think rabbits and hares were part of the rodent family. Now they know these animals are part of a different family. Rabbits and hares are one family of lagomorphs.

Snowshoe hare
in winter

Now You Know!

A snowshoe hare has such thick fur on its feet that it can walk on top of snow, just like a person wearing snowshoes.

Mammals are also covered with fur or hair. Rabbits and hares have short, soft fur. They even have fur on the bottom of their feet! Most rabbits and hares are brown or gray. Some of them change color in the winter. The snowshoe hare lives where there is a lot of snow. In winter, its fur changes to white. That white fur helps the snowshoe hare blend in with its white surroundings. It is great **camouflage**!

A brown snowshoe hare blends in with the woods during the summer.

Size and Shape

Size is one way to tell rabbits and hares apart. Hares are bigger than rabbits. A hare can weigh up to 15 pounds (7 kg). They can be up to two feet (60 cm) long.

Holland lop rabbit

Most rabbits are small. Most wild rabbits weigh between one and four pounds. The smallest rabbit is called the pygmy rabbit. It weighs less than one pound and is only 9 to 11 inches (22–28 cm) long.

Some people breed rabbits to keep as pets. These rabbits can be much bigger than wild rabbits. A Flemish giant rabbit weighs over 20 pounds (9 kg) and can be up to 32 inches (81 cm) long!

Columbia basin pygmy rabbit

Flemish giant rabbit

Another way to tell hares and rabbits apart is the shape of their bodies. Both hares and rabbits have long legs. However, a hare's legs are a lot longer than a rabbit's. Those long legs mean that hares are really good jumpers.

Hares and rabbits jump by bringing their long back legs up to their front legs. Then they push forward with their back legs. A hare can jump up to 20 feet (6 m) in a single move.

Both hares and rabbits also have long ears that stick up. A hare's ears are longer than a rabbit's. A hare often has black or dark fur on the tip of its ears as well.

NOW YOU KNOW!

The antelope jackrabbit's ears are almost one-third the length of its body.

Hare ears

Rabbit ears

Hare running in a meadow

13

Staying Safe

Those long legs and ears help rabbits and hares stay safe. Many **predators** like to eat rabbits and hares. These predators include foxes, weasels, badgers, coyotes, wolves, bobcats, raccoons, hawks, and snakes. Sometimes **domestic** cats and dogs kill rabbits.

A rabbit or hare's long ears help them hear if a predator is coming. A rabbit or hare will sit very still with its ears sticking straight up. If the animal hears a scary sound, it quickly runs away. A rabbit or hare has ears that are shaped like cups. This shape helps capture sounds and gives these animals very good hearing.

A desert cottontail
rabbit keeps on the
alert in northern
Arizona.

Siamese rabbit running across a meadow

Jackrabbit running through a field

When a rabbit or hare hears something scary, it's time to run away! A hare can jump far with its long back legs. Hares can also move very fast. A hare can jump away at 40 miles (64 km) an hour.

Rabbits are fast too. A rabbit cannot jump as far as a hare. But it kicks its back legs off the ground as it runs. This kick helps a rabbit run fast and cover a lot of ground in one leap.

Rabbits also change direction as they run. They **swerve** left and right. These quick movements make it hard for a predator to catch them.

Homes All Over the World

Hares and rabbits live all over the world. They live on every continent except Antarctica. These animals can live in hot places and cold places. Many rabbits live in the woods or in grassy fields. More than half the rabbit species in the world live in North America.

The jackrabbit is a hare, even though its name sounds like a rabbit. Jackrabbits live in the western part of the United States and Canada. They also live in Mexico. Some of these hares live in a hot, dry desert habitat. Others live in the **tundra**, where it is always cold.

Now You Know!

The swamp rabbit lives in the southern United States. Most rabbits don't like water, but the swamp rabbit often swims away from predators.

This black tailed jackrabbit makes its home in southeastern Arizona.

Rabbits are good at digging burrows and tunnels.

This happy rabbit is enjoying its new burrow.

Making a Home

Another way to tell hares and rabbits apart is the kind of home they make. Rabbits like to dig. They dig **burrows** in the ground. These burrows can include many dens and tunnels. Sometimes rabbits dig burrows that are connected to each other. A large group of rabbit burrows is called a warren.

Hares do not dig burrows. Instead, they push down grass to make a hollow that is big enough for their body. These hollows are called *forms*. They make a good home on top of the ground in the desert, tundra, or open plains.

A nountain hare takes shelter in a form.

Time to Eat!

Both hares and rabbits are **herbivores**. They only eat plants. When the weather is warm, rabbits eat grass, weeds, flowers, and garden plants. When the weather gets cold, they eat twigs, buds, and tree bark. Hares also eat grass. They like fruit, seeds, and vegetables too.

Hares and rabbits are **nocturnal**. They sleep during most of the day. They wake up and come outside in the evening. Then it is time to find food. Hares like to live alone, but rabbits live and eat in groups.

A black tailed jackrabbit gets a mouthful of tree leaves.

A wild rabbit eating grass

Lots of Babies

Rabbits and hares give birth to a lot of babies. A female rabbit or hare is called a doe. A male is called a buck. Does and bucks mate in the early spring. Rabbits give birth about 30 days later. Hares give birth after about 42 days. Both hares and rabbits can have several **litters** every year.

Newborn dwarf dutch rabbits in a nest

Baby rabbits are called kittens. A rabbit can give birth to up to nine kittens at a time. Kittens are tiny and have very little fur. They are blind and deaf and cannot walk. Their mother hides them in her burrow and takes care of them. After only 16 days, the kittens can leave the burrow. A young rabbit can start having its own babies when it is just four months old.

Newborn rabbits

Now You Know!

Only one in ten baby rabbits will live to adulthood. Most of the others are eaten by predators.

A female hare gives birth to about six babies at a time. Baby hares are called **leverets**. Leverets can hop and walk just a few minutes after they are born. They can see and hear and they have fur. Each leveret makes its own form soon after it is born.

But leverets still need their mother. The mother hops from one leveret to another to **nurse** them. About four weeks later, the leverets are ready to live on their own.

Arctic hare nursing leverets

Leveret hare lying down in a meadow

Leveret hare

Too Many Rabbits?

Rabbits **reproduce** quickly. They also eat a lot. For these reasons, rabbits can turn into pests. Too many rabbits can destroy a **habitat**.

There were no rabbits in Australia until Europeans brought them during the 1800s. Within a few years, there were billions of rabbits running wild in Australia. They damaged crops and wild plants. They stole burrows from native animals and ate their food. The Australian government has tried to stop the spread of rabbits, but nothing they do has worked.

In other places in the world, some rabbits are **endangered**. They have lost their habitats. Sometimes they are killed by polluted water or food. Many groups are trying to save endangered rabbits and hares.

Important Animals

Rabbits and hares are important parts of our natural world. They provide a food source for many other animals. They also eat plants and help keep  nature in balance. Hares and rabbits may look a lot alike, but they are not the same! Each one is a special and unique creature that is part of life on Earth.

Now You Know!

Many people keep domestic rabbits as pets. However, hares are too wild and do not make good pets.

Glossary

burrow a hole dug by a small animal

camouflage coloring or markings on an animal's skin that help it blend in with its surroundings

domestic raised or kept by people

endangered in danger of dying out

habitat a place where animals and plants live

herbivores animals that only eat plants

leveret a baby hare

litters groups of babies born at the same time

mammals animals that have backbones and fur or hair, are warm-blooded, and give birth to live young

nocturnal active at night

nurse to feed a baby with milk from the mother's body

predators animals that hunt other animals for food

reproduce to give birth

swerve to change direction very quickly

tundra an area in the Arctic where the ground is always frozen

Read More in the Library

Armentrout, David. *Raising Rabbits*. Rourke, 2011.